The Educator's Guide to Creating Connections

CORWIN CONNECTED EDUCATORS SERIES

Worlds of Making: Best Practices for Establishing a Makerspace for Your School
By Laura Fleming @NMHS_lms

Personalized Learning Plans for Teachers
By Tom Murray @thomascmurray and Jeff Zoul @Jeff_Zoul

Empowered Schools, Empowered Students: Creating Connected and Invested Learners
By Pernille Ripp @pernilleripp

Blogging for Educators: Tips for Getting Connected
By Starr Sackstein @mssackstein

Principal PD
By Joseph Sanfelippo @Joesanfelippofc and Tony Sinanis @TonySinanis

The Power of Branding: Telling Your School's Story
By Tony Sinanis @TonySinanis and Joseph Sanfelippo @Joesanfelippofc

The Educator's Guide to Creating Connections
Edited by Tom Whitby @tomwhitby

The Relevant Educator: How Connectedness Empowers Learning
By Tom Whitby @tomwhitby and Steven W. Anderson @web20classroom

The Educator's Guide to Creating Connections

Tom Whitby, Editor

CORWIN
A SAGE Company

A SAGE Company

FOR INFORMATION:

Corwin

A SAGE Company

2455 Teller Road

Thousand Oaks, California 91320

(800) 233-9936

www.corwin.com

SAGE Publications Ltd.

1 Oliver's Yard

55 City Road

London EC1Y 1SP

United Kingdom

SAGE Publications India Pvt. Ltd.

B 1/I 1 Mohan Cooperative Industrial Area

Mathura Road, New Delhi 110 044

India

SAGE Publications Asia-Pacific Pte. Ltd.

3 Church Street

#10-04 Samsung Hub

Singapore 049483

Copyright © 2016 by Corwin

Printed in the United States of America

ISBN 978-1-4833-9288-2

This book is printed on acid-free paper.

Acquisitions Editor: Ariel Price

Editorial Assistant: Andrew Olson

Production Editor: Amy Schroller

Copy Editor: Cate Huisman

Typesetter: C&M Digitals (P) Ltd.

Proofreader: Rae-Ann Goodwin

Cover and Interior Designer: Janet Kiesel

Marketing Manager: Lisa Lysne

Certified Chain of Custody
SUSTAINABLE   Promoting Sustainable Forestry
FORESTRY
INITIATIVE   www.sfiprogram.org
SFI-01268
SFI label applies to text stock

15 16 17 18 19 10 9 8 7 6 5 4 3 2 1

Contents

Preface

My best friend is a high school math teacher. When I started working on the Corwin Connected Educators series, I excitedly told her about the power of using social media to connect with other educators. I passed on what I learned from the authors in this series: that the greatest resource educators have is each other. At a conference, she heard Jennie Magiera speak and finally made the leap to getting on Twitter. Although I wasn't sure she would continue tweeting, she did, and even joined Twitter chats like #connectedtl and #slowmathchat. A few days later she texted me saying, "I seriously cannot thank you enough. You have changed my life."

Being "connected" seems deceptively simple: Just get on Twitter, right? But that's really not enough. For those who truly embrace connectedness, it's a lifestyle change, an openness to sharing and learning in an entirely new environment. We're seeing the impact of this shift in mindset worldwide. Policies are changing, new jobs in education are being created, hitherto impossible collaborations are happening, pedagogy is evolving, and there's a heightened awareness of each person's individual impact. All of these changes are explored in the Connected Educators series.

While you can see the full list of books on the series page, we're introducing several new books to the series; they will be published in the fall of 2015 and spring of 2016. These books each contribute something unique and necessary not only for educators who are new to the world of connected education but also for those who have been immersed in it for some time.

Tom Whitby, coauthor of *The Relevant Educator,* has brought together a group of experienced connected educators in his new book, *The Educator's Guide to Creating Connections.* Contributors Pam Moran, George Couros, Kyle Pace, Adam Bellow, Lisa Nielsen, Kristen Swanson, Steven Anderson, and Shannon McClintock Miller discuss the ways that connectedness has impacted them and the benefits it can have for all educators—policy makers, school and district leaders, and teachers.

While all connected educators are evangelists for being connected, connectedness does not necessarily prevent common problems, such as isolation in leadership. In *Breaking Out of Isolation,* Spike Cook, Jessica Johnson, and Theresa Stager explain how connectedness can alleviate the loneliness leaders can feel in their position and also, when used effectively, help leaders maintain balance in their lives and stay motivated.

For districts and schools embracing the connected mindset and empowering all of their learners to use technology, a solid plan for digital citizenship is a must. In *Digital Citizenship,* Susan Bearden provides a look at how leaders can prepare teachers and students for the new responsibilities of using technology and interacting with others on a truly global platform.

Connected education provides unique opportunities for teachers in their classrooms as well. In *Standing in the Gap,* Lisa Dabbs and Nicol Howard explore the ways that social media can specifically help new teachers find resources, connect to mentors, and encourage each other in their careers. Erin Klein, Tom Murray, A. J. Juliani, and Ben Gilpin show how teachers can purposefully integrate technology and empower their students in both physical and digital classrooms in *Redesigning Learning Spaces.*

One of the most powerful impacts connected education can have is in reaching marginalized populations. In *Confident Voices,* John Spencer shows how social media and other technology tools can empower English language learners. Billy Krakower and Sharon LePage Plante have also discovered that technology can reach special and gifted learners as well.

The books in the Corwin Connected Educators series are supported by a companion website featuring videos, articles, downloadable forms, and other resources to help you as you start and continue your journey. Best of all, the authors in the series want to connect with *you!* We've provided their Twitter handles and other contact information on the companion website.

Once you've taken the step to joining a network, don't stop there. Share what you're doing; you never know when it will help someone else!

—*Peter DeWitt, Series Editor*
@PeterMDeWitt

—*Ariel Price, Associate Editor*
@arielkprice

About the Editor

**Tom Whitby** is the coauthor of *The Relevant Educator: How Connectedness Empowers Learning.* He is @tomwhitby on Twitter and has 61,000 followers. Whitby retired from public education after serving 34 years as a secondary English teacher, and he spent an additional six years as an adjunct professor of education at St. Joseph's College in New York. He is a cocreator of #Edchat, an award-winning education discussion group on Twitter. He is an education blogger for My Island View: Educational, Disconnected Utterances, as well as a blogger for Edutopia. The Qatar Foundation has invited him for the past three years to attend the WISE Conference, an international education conference in Doha, Qatar. He hosts the weekly Edchat radio show on the BAM radio network. He created the Educator's PLN, a global Ning site, where approximately 17,000+ educators share and collaborate daily. He is the founder of seven educational groups on LinkedIn, the largest being the Technology-Using Professors Group, which has 14,000+ members. He has been a member of the US Department of Education's planning committee for Connected Educator Month since 2012. Whitby served as a contributing editor while developing SmartBlog on Education by SmartBrief, and he has written about social media in education for several national education journals, including *Learning and Leading,* the journal of the International Society for Technology in Education. He has presented at statewide and national and international education

conferences, including the Florida Educational Technology Conference (FETC) and the conferences of the ASCD, International Society for Technical Education (ISTE), Texas Computer Education Association (TCEA), New York State Association for Computers and Technologies in Education (NYSCATE), Michigan Association of Computer Users in Learning (MACUL), Illinois Computing Educators (ICE), Software & Information Industry Association (SIIA), as well as several 140 Character Conferences on social media in Los Angeles and New York City.

About the Contributors

Steven W. Anderson is a learner, blogger, speaker, educational evangelist, author, and Dad. As a former teacher and director of instructional technology, he is highly sought after for his expertise in educational technology integration and using social media for learning. As @web20classroom, he regularly travels the country talking to schools and districts about the use of social media in the classroom and how they can better serve students through technology. Steven has been a presenter and keynoter at several education technology conferences, including those of the ISTE, ASCD, FETC, and Virginia Society for Technology in Education (VSTE) as well as numerous state and local conferences. With Tom Whitby, he is coauthor of *The Relevant Educator: How Connectedness Empowers Learning* (Corwin, 2014). He was also responsible for helping create #Edchat, a weekly education discussion on Twitter that boasts over 500 weekly participants. Steven has been recognized with the 2009 and 2011 Edublog Twitterer of the Year awards, a Microsoft Heroes of Education award, and a 2013 Bammy award, recognized worldwide as the educational Emmy, for his work with #Edchat.

Adam Bellow has worked as a classroom teacher, technology training specialist, and senior director of technology for the College Board Schools. He is also the founder and CEO of eduTecher, eduClipper,

 and WeLeanedIt, web and app resources designed for teachers and students. Adam has been working to have a positive impact on the educational technology community for many years. He is the coauthor of the book *Untangling the Web* (Faber & Faber, 2013) and has been a presenter at many conferences since, including ISTE, #140edu, TEDxNYED, and many others. Adam has received numerous awards for his work in education, including the Outstanding Young Educator award from ISTE and the Making IT Happen award.

 **George Couros** is the division principal of innovative teaching and learning for Parkland School Division and an innovative learning and leadership consultant. He has worked at all levels of schooling, from kindergarten through high school, as a teacher, technology facilitator, and school administrator. He is a sought-after speaker on the topic of innovative student learning and engagement and has worked with schools and organizations all over the world. George is also the creator of Connected Principals, the founder of Connected Canada, and the School Admin Virtual Mentor Program (#SAVMP). His focus is to help organizations create optimal learning environments for innovation within schools.

 **Shannon McClintock Miller** is a teacher, librarian, and technology integration specialist. She encourages young people and educators to have a voice while learning, creating, collaborating, and connecting to others globally. She is an educational consultant for Mackin Educational Resources, director of school and library strategy for In This Together Media, and executive director of library and educational services for Biblionasium.

Shannon speaks and consults in Iowa and around the country on education, librarianship, technology, social media, and making a difference in education and the lives of others. She is the author of the award-winning The Library Voice blog and enjoys writing for various blogs, journals, and other forums.

Shannon is a member of American Library Association (ALA), American Association of School Librarians (AASL), Iowa Association of School Librarians (IASL), Iowa Library Association (ILA), ISTE, Special Interest Group Media Specialists (SIGMS), ASCD, and the Children's Literature Network, and she is on the board of directors of the Iowa Student Learning Institute. She serves on AASL's Best Websites committee and STEM Task Force; and on advisory boards for *Library Journal, Horn Book, School Library Journal, School Library Monthly,* Rosen Digital Library, StarWalk Kids, EasyBib, BiblioNasium, eSchool Media, Gale K12 Customer, and In This Together Media. She is a FableVision ambassador, social media WRADvocate for LitWorld's World Read Aloud Day, and part of the Bammy Awards Council of Peers. She has served as advocacy chair for IASL and on the advisory council for the Iowa Center for the Book Advisory Council.

In 2011, Shannon was awarded the Connecting People Shorty Award, and in 2012, she was chosen to be part of the SLJ New Leaders Program. In 2013, she was named one of the Faces of Innovation by Broadband for America, she was one of 50 featured in the 2013 Center for Digital Education Yearbook, and she was one of the featured Connected Educators with the Connected Educators projects partnered with the US Department of Education. In 2014, Shannon was named a *Library Journal* Mover & Shaker.

Pam Moran, superintendent of Albemarle County Public Schools in Virginia, has been a middle school science teacher, elementary principal, and assistant superintendent. She has served as a president of the Virginia Association of School Superintendents and of the Women Educational Leaders of Virginia. She currently serves as a board member of the State Higher Education Council for Virginia and is a past member of the American Association of School Administrators (AASA) governing board. Recognized as a national Tech Savvy Superintendent in 2010 and recipient of the Bammy Superintendent's Award in 2013, she has presented and keynoted at numerous state and national conferences, including those of the National School Boards Association (NSBA), ISTE, VSTE, TIE-Co, VitaLearn-VT, the Digital Media and Learning Research Hub, EduCon, Oregon Instructional Technologies Strategies Conference, the School Library Journal, the Consortium for School Networking, Virginia ASCD, Interactive College of Technology–Tipperary, TEDx, and more. Active in social media, she has blogged for AASA, EDSurge, Edleader21, MakerEd, Edurati Review, Cooperative Catalysts, and Connected Superintendents as well as for her school district and at her own personal site, A Space for Learning (https://spacesforlearning.wordpress.com/). She currently cohosts Change Ed for Bam Radio. She believes the stories of the learners and educators whom she serves provide hope for the future of public education and are important to share.

Lisa Nielsen found school boring and irrelevant when she was a student. That ticked her off, so she became a public school educator who works to help change that for others. She does this by finding and sharing innovative ways to prepare students for relevant and real-world success. Among other things, this means ensuring educators and students have a voice in conversations, issues, and policies that affect them.

She began her career in the 1990s as a librarian, which was a perfect fit, enabling her to create a buzzing and vibrant oasis in Harlem where students could find their passions with support from the community. Since then she has served in various capacities including as a literacy coach, ed tech professional development manager, and technology innovation manager. Today she serves as the director of digital literacy and citizenship for New York City schools. Lisa has been recognized for her work, receiving awards such as Teacher of the Year by her district and most recently the International Society of Technology Educator's Making IT Happen award.

Lisa writes for and speaks to audiences across the globe about the future of education, but she is best known for her award-winning blog, The Innovative Educator (http://theinnovativeeducator.blog spot.com).Her writing and work are also featured in publications and on the Internet in *The New York Times, THE Journal, Tech & Learning Magazine,* SmartBlogs, ISTE Connects, *The Huffington Post,* and Answers.com, as well as on ASCD's The Whole Child website and on the websites of MindShift and Leading & Learning. She is the author of the book *Teaching Generation Text* (Jossey-Bass, 2011).

Kyle Pace, an instructional technology specialist, has worked with K–12 teachers in his current school district to provide instructional technology professional development for the last 11 years, and he has prior experience in the elementary classroom. Kyle champions the support of teaching and learning with meaningful technology integration using a multitude of educational technologies.

Kyle speaks at education conferences such as ASCD, Learning Forward, ISTE, and FETC. Kyle also speaks and presents virtually for groups such as the Simple K12 Teacher Learning Community and at conferences such as those of *Education Week.*

Kyle coauthored a book titled *Integrating Technology With Music Instruction* (Alfred Music, 2009). Kyle has also organized all five annual Edcamp KC "unconferences" since 2010.

In July 2011, Kyle was one of 50 educators from around the world chosen to participate in the Google Teacher Academy in Seattle, Washington, to become a Google Certified Teacher. In January 2013, Kyle was named as one of *Education Week's* 2013 Leaders to Learn From and joined the other honorees in April 2013 in Washington, DC to receive special recognition from Secretary of

Education Arne Duncan. Kyle was also selected to join the 2013 ASCD class of Emerging Leaders.

Kyle has a strong passion for sharing with teachers, administrators, students, and parents about the impact that educational technology can have on adult and student learning.

Kristen Swanson, EdD, helps teachers design meaningful interactive curricula at the local and national levels. She has taught at the elementary level, served as a regional consultant for Response to Intervention (a school-based, multilevel intervention system to maximize student achievement and reduce behavior problems), and worked as an educational technology director for a public school district in Pennsylvania. She holds a BA degree from DeSales University, two MA degrees from Wilkes University, and an EdD degree from Widener University. Kristen is currently an adjunct in the DeSales University instructional technology MEd program and a senior research leader for BrightBytes, a data analytics platform that measures the use of technology and links it to learning outcomes.

Kristen is passionate about meaningful professional learning. She currently serves as a member of the Edcamp Foundation board and is chair of the longstanding Edcamp Foundation Partner Program. She has shared her ideas and expertise at ASCD conferences, TEDxPhiladelphiaED, TEDxNYED, and Educon. She has also published in academic journals, including *Literacy Learning: The Middle Years* and the *Journal of Reading, Writing, and Literacy*. She is the author of *Professional Learning in the Digital Age: The Educator's Guide to User-Generated Learning* (Routledge, 2012), *Unleashing Student Superpowers* (Corwin, 2014), and *Teaching the Common Core Speaking and Listening Standards* (Routledge, 2013).

Kristen is active in the educational technology sphere. She is a Google Certified Teacher, Twitter teacher, Edublog award nominee, and avid blogger. She strongly believes that rigorous curriculum fosters meaningful technology integration, and she is also interested in the learning opportunities provided by asynchronous learning.

Introduction

I n the initial stages of the development of this book, I assembled
from my collegial connections people who I felt could best
instruct educators about the many things a relevant educator
should know in order to excel at developing pedagogy and methodology for learners in the 21st century.

In a profession that deals with information and knowledge as commodities to be imparted and shared, it is very apparent that each
of those commodities is evolving at a pace never before experienced in history, and that technology has had a profound effect on
the speed of this evolution. This challenges educators today to find
ways to keep up with this evolution in order to prepare students
for a world that will not look like the world in which they grew up.
Just consider all of the changes that have taken place over the
13 years since students in this year's high school graduating classes
entered into their academic careers.

The challenge to modern educators goes way beyond the require-
ment that they be both content experts and education experts, as
was required of educators in past centuries. A third area of expertise
for today's educator requires the ability to adapt in order to stay
relevant. This requires a basic and ongoing knowledge of technology
literacy and awareness of how things fit together within a modern
learning environment.

All of this can be overwhelming to those educators unfamiliar with
the ways of connected collaboration, or using technology to collaborate with other educators locally, nationally, and globally.

Again, this was never possible to this extent in education in centuries past. There are a great many things that educators can do to begin to tap into a network of collegial connections. They can also use their technology along with these new connections to develop methodologies to address new pedagogies that are ever evolving in our computer-driven culture.

Assembled to write this book are teachers, administrators, consultants, and even a "40 years in the classroom" retired teacher—educators all. All are experts in the areas that they address in the book. The questions we were asked were the following: With this much diversity in the various levels of content, to whom is this book directed? Who is the audience? Is it for administrators, teachers, or someone else?

I toyed with the idea of using the term *lead learner,* which has been bouncing around with connected educators for a while. Originally, it referred to building principals, but today it now seems to be evolving to standout educators as well. Even the term *connected educators* is fairly new to the profession, even after being recognized by the US Department of Education three years ago with its Connected Educator Month.

I think any educator of today needs more than anything to have a "growth mindset." Today's educator should have the ability to continue to learn and try new and different things; to embrace failure as a learning experience; to communicate, collaborate, and share with other educators; and to see the big picture of education in order to innovate and affect change. This would apply to any educator, teacher, or administrator. Educators need to apply the lifelong learner philosophy to themselves as seriously as they profess it to their students.

This book is applicable for any educator or administrator seeking relevance in a profession that now requires it. Educators must now be flexible and adaptive with tools of technology to evolve as teachers, and they must have an understanding of technology to show their students how to evolve as learners. Administrators and educators will benefit from an awareness of the potential technology has to advance pedagogy and methodology. They must have an understanding that develops both, so that we are not trying to use 20th century methods with 21st century tools and wondering why it doesn't work.

My answer therefore is that this book is for any educator who is seeking relevance in a world of education that requires more change than has ever been required before of educators. It is for any educator—administrator or teacher—who is looking for suggestions for a solid pathway to relevance. The diplomas and licenses of the past are not enough to carry educators through their entire careers. If professional development of the past centuries worked, we would not be involved in a national, or now global, discussion on education reform. Taking control of one's learning is a daunting task, but we have the technology to do just that.

It is hoped that this book will be a starting point for educators to begin to create their own sources for learning, as well as to develop sources for their students in a world where technology will provide constant pressure for change. This change will require constant adaptation and flexibility for the teacher as well as the learner.

Tom Whitby @tomwhitby

Personalized Learning

Tom Whitby @tomwhitby

WHAT IS COLLABORATION TODAY?

Collaboration has been with us from the time people started learning. For many people, it is the method of learning that works best for them. Historically, collaborative learning had its limitations. For the most part it could only take place in face-to-face encounters. The collaborative parties needed to be in the same location at the same time for collaboration to be most effective. I am sure that there were successful collaborative efforts that took place through the mail, or over telephone lines, but that was costly in both time and money. The real game-changer, however, came with the advance of the Internet and social media applications (apps).

Technology has allowed us to bypass the boundaries of time and space, so that we can now collaborate anywhere in the world at almost any time with consideration of global time zones. Face-to-face applications like Apple Facetime, Skype, and Google Hangout allow collaborators to view each other, as well as source materials, for collaboration. Google Drive enables real-time collaborative editing of documents, spreadsheets, graphs, and diagrams, so that several collaborators may work on the same document simultaneously in real-time collaboration.

With the element of collaboration now so seamlessly woven into the fabric of learning through technology, it becomes more than just a consumption of content. Learning becomes a collaborative creation of content, which is also shared out with others. We no longer need to seek out that one educated individual who serves as a content expert, whose purpose is to fill our empty vessel with knowledge that he or she determines we may need. We can find and join many people to work together in creating the very content that we specifically need. We take control of our own learning. It becomes a group effort in sharing content that begins to fill that empty vessel, and not only do we get partake of our own learning, we also get to direct it.

WHY SHOULD I COLLABORATE?

It is through collaboration that we can personalize our learning to meet our needs using connected colleagues as sources for our learning. A connected colleague would be someone we connected to through social media, or it could be a face-to-face connection as well. These people become members of our personal or professional learning network. After several years of using this term, I now call it my *personalized learning network* (PLN). What I love about collaboration is that in a room full of smart collaborative individuals, the smartest one there is the room itself. Collectively, we are all smarter than we are individually. That is the power behind collaborative learning. We can direct our learning to whatever it is we determine we need to know, personally or professionally. An advantage of collaboration is exposure to the experience and knowledge of others. We don't know what it is that we don't know. Sharing experiences gives us access to the learning of others, who provide their experiences to expand our knowledge.

WITH WHOM SHOULD I COLLABORATE?

In order to reap the benefits of collaborative learning, one must first develop a network of collegial sources. Teachers already have established collegial sources in their departments, schools, and districts. For whatever number of colleagues as one may have "in house," that number is dwarfed by the potential number of global connections. Many of the people available through the Internet include the very thought leaders, authors, bloggers, and lead learners that are driving education discussions around the world. In creating this network, each individual selects the people with whom he or she wants to connect. Select the best people in order to get the best results. Good people are vocal, articulate, informed, involved, and most importantly have a collaborative spirit. Titles are secondary to ideas. Just because a person is a superintendent of a school district, a director, or a principal, that does not ensure that she or he has great ideas in education. Many educators have a mindset that dwells in the 20th century. Moving backward does not work well when we are educating kids for their future. Great ideas come from many individuals, and some may not have titles or degrees.

WARNING: DO NOT GET OVERWHELMED!

With an understanding of why we should connect with others for collaboration, we need to now get into how to do it. This is the part where many people have trouble. It requires the use of technology, a scary proposition for many. Do not be overwhelmed by the overview of how to connect presented in this book, and especially by those overviews given by enthusiastic (sometimes overachieving) connected educators. This can be daunting if you believe that it will all happen in a day. Becoming connected and developing a collaborative mindset are processes, not the result of reading a book. It will take time. You need to do one or two things well, and then move on to the next one or two. The worst advocate for being a connected educator is a connected educator. They scare people with their extensive lists of connected accomplishments.

And in the end it comes down to you—the user—the teacher. You live and teach in an amazing time. And your students

> Becoming connected and developing a collaborative mindset are processes, not the result of reading a book.

learn in an amazing time. Using these new tools can seem like more work at times. Sometimes things won't work the way you want. But that is true of traditional teaching methods too.

Collaborative people are found everywhere on social media. For most educators, entry into the world of social media was for the sole purpose of collaboration. It has been my experience that many, if not most, educators feel a moral obligation to share ideas. It is part of the makeup of an educator. They are collaborative, if not by nature, by a lifetime of learning and sharing as a student and then as a teacher.

Education blogs are a great source of connections for educators. Commenting supportively on blogs develops relationships, encouraging further connections. Conversing and commenting with educators on Twitter, LinkedIn, Facebook, or Pinterest can yield contacts with any number of educators who will add great value to your network. On apps like Twitter, educators frequently recommend good educators to follow and connect. There are sites like Facebook and LinkedIn that host education discussions and education groups. These are also sources for connections. A collaborative educator on social media begins to look for opportunities to connect and develop relationships with other interested educators.

HOW DO I DEVELOP A PLN FOR COLLABORATION?

The key to directing authentic, collaborative learning for professional and personal development is to establish a PLN. Each PLN is unique to its owner. Since each network is made up of individuals that the owner determined would help in her or his personal learning, each of those PLN members is a personal choice. Additionally, access to those individuals can come from a myriad of applications that the collaborators share. Consequently, whom we connect with and how we connect with him or her forces each PLN to be unique to each owner. This makes for truly personalized learning.

There is one application however that is shared by most connected educators: Twitter. Educators have taken Twitter beyond the use that was envisioned by its creators. It has become more than just a whimsical sharing of social experiences. It enables educators to share in a concise form the information most needed for collaboration. Documents, articles, posts, videos, podcasts, websites, discussions, photos, diagrams, spreadsheets, and just ideas can all be instantly shared either individually or globally.

HOW DO I GET STARTED WITH A PLN?

For most connected educators, Twitter has become the backbone of the PLN. It is the primary source used to share information and content. There are Twitter strategies for increasing the number of connections to one's PLN through recommendations from other educators. Twitter can be used to direct traffic to any site an individual wants to share.

I often tell people that trying to teach Twitter by explaining it is similar to trying to teach swimming in a gymnasium. One needs to get into the pool to learn to swim, as much as one needs to be on Twitter in order to learn how to tweet. The beauty of learning about Twitter while using it is that there are many people on Twitter who will extend themselves to help you along.

The concept of Twitter is simple: One shares things using up to 140 characters in a text message called a *tweet*. All users on Twitter follow (are connected to) people and in turn have people follow (be connected to) them. It does not need to be reciprocal. People could be followers without having to be followed back. Simply stated, the only people who will read your tweets will be the people who follow you. If you have 10 followers, your tweets will go only to them. If any of those 10 people put out a tweet, you will see it only if you are following them as well. If you are not following them, you will not see their tweets. You may follow or unfollow anyone at any time. There are no notifications sent to those whom you unfollow. Every tweet you send out is received by only your followers, but tweets may also be accessed by the public, since they are displayed on your Twitter profile. This requires a knowledge of getting around in Twitter, but it is easily done. You must be thoughtful about what you tweet.

> Every Tweet sent out is publicly displayed, so be thoughtful about what you tweet.

The only private message is a direct message (DM). You can send a DM to those who you follow only if they, in turn, follow you as well.

Following people is how you build a valuable PLN. If you follow people that you value in education, then you will build a valuable PLN. If you follow entertainers, sports folks, friends, and cousins, then your network becomes something different from a PLN.

My Twitter handle is @tomwhitby. I use my name because I am using Twitter professionally, and people need to know who I am. Some educators select pseudonyms for Twitter. My Twitter profile explains who I am as an educator, and has my avatar, the displayed picture or animation used to identify the tweeter. I want people to see that I am a professional so that they follow me knowing I am there for education. I check out other's profiles before I follow them to make the same determination.

Going to people's profiles enables you to see the types of tweets they send out. You will also have access to folks that they follow as well as lists they may have made to categorize those that they follow. These are all sources for you to follow, building your PLN. Another great source for follows would be education bloggers whom you find insightful. Most bloggers have "Follow Me on Twitter" buttons on their sites for an easy follow.

Education chats are a very big part of the Twitter culture. There are hundreds of chats or real-time discussions taking place on Twitter daily (Google search: education chat schedule). Entering into these chats not only expands learning but also offers up more valuable people to follow for further engagement and collaboration. These chats are followed through the use of hashtags (#).

Hashtags extend the range of a tweet. One of the most common education hashtags is #Edchat. Educators will attach it at the end of a tweet to alert people that it is an education worthy tweet. If a tweeter has 10 followers, then her or his tweets go to only 10 people. When the #Edchat hashtag is added to a tweet, that tweet travels to thousands of educators who follow the hashtag #Edchat. This exposes the tweeter to more potential followers. It is also possible to do hashtag searches, or create a column to follow specific hashtags.

The very best way to build up a following of educators is through the use of the retweet (RT). When a really smart tweet appears in your timeline, you can tweet it out again as a retweet. It then is shared with people following you. It credits the original tweeter as well as you. The power of the RT is that if you concentrate on retweeting really smart or valuable tweets, people assume you, the retweeter, are really smart and want to follow you.

There are several applications other than Twitter that will enable better organization of tweets that may interest you. Tweetdeck and Hootsuite both allow the creation of columns to follow specific individuals, groups, or hashtags. The mobile versions of these apps seem far less efficient than the desktop versions.

These are the basics of Twitter. Once an educator is using Twitter, the very people that are followed become mentors. It is again all part of that collaborative mindset. Once they join Twitter, most people lurk for a short period of time, learning the culture and mechanics of Twitter. To lurk, in the Twitter culture, is to observe without interacting. It is quietly observing. After a period of lurking and learning, actual engagement with other tweeters and then real learning begins. It requires a commitment to leave a comfort zone for many, but the rewards are beyond expectation for most educators.

The idea of being a connected, collaborative educator is a concept that did not exist 10 years ago. It is also a mindset and a way of life. It is truly a path to the lifelong learning that educators have been talking about for so long. It will not happen in the short term but over a period of time. It takes but 20 minutes a day to be connected. Once they have gotten connected, however, connected educators will experience a joy in self-directed learning that they probably have not experienced before. It will be pleasurable spending more time connecting and learning. There will be an easy transfer of that learning to the profession of education, which benefits students and colleagues alike. To better educate our children, we must first better educate their educators.

Three Take-Aways

1. Begin to "follow" educators on Twitter. Look at the profiles of those educators you follow, and then follow the educators that they follow.

2. Visit the site Teach 100 at www.teach100.com. It will provide a comprehensive list of education blogs to follow. Select one blog each week, and share it by tweeting its link to colleagues. Additionally, follow the blogger on Twitter.

3. Join at least one education chat a week to actively participate in a discussion on education. Find the most interesting contributors, and follow them on Twitter.

Digitally Enhanced Leadership

Kyle Pace @kylepace

W hat is a digitally enhanced leader? It sort of sounds like a half human, half robot, doesn't it? Not quite. Digitally enhanced leaders equip themselves with knowledge of digital tools that are appropriate for various tasks. These tasks tend to fall under umbrellas such as these:

- communication
- collaboration
- curation
- creativity

Does a leader's use of technology have to be constant? Of course not—just as technology does not need to be constantly infused into classroom learning. The use of technology should be appropriate for the work at hand. It should be purposeful. Just as it is in classrooms, the focus should remain on learning first; administrators and teacher leaders should keep this focus when looking to redefine an existing task with technology.

Why digital literacy for school, district, and teacher leaders? The reason is the same as for any other initiative or new idea that preceded technology. A good leader does not ask anyone to try something that the leader is not willing to try. In my school district, some of the strongest success I've seen with forward movement of educational technology is when there was a concerted effort to bring growth to district, building, and teacher leadership first. The by-product of this was what I like to call a "trickle down" effect. By raising awareness and increasing capacity in our district, building, and school leadership, our digitally fluent leaders piqued staff interest, which opened doors to do the same for more teachers, which led to more use with students. So, how did we do this? What did we cover? If you go back to those 4Cs mentioned earlier, I believe those become the tenets of a digitally enhanced leader.

COMMUNICATION

Communication is at the heart of a leader. Some administrators would argue that good communication with staff, parents, and the community is everything. So how does a district or a school leader use digitally enhanced communication? What are some strategies that you could try tomorrow?

Remind

Remind (www.remind.com) is a fantastic free service teachers and leaders can use to communicate with students and parents easily and efficiently. Administrators can use this as a great way to communicate with staff and/or parents. Messages via Remind are sent as text messages; however, neither the sender nor the receiver of the messages ever sees anyone's phone number. Users can set up groups (classes) easily, and subscribing to receive updates is equally easy. Remind is a fast, efficient way for district and school leaders to communicate key information right to the device that parents and students use most.

Blogs

If you're looking to publish a piece of writing of more length along with all the formatting options you've likely become accustomed to, then blogging might be a better fit for some you. We're in a time when most teachers are either required or strongly encouraged to have some type of web presence for their classroom; for a principal, creating a principal's blog is a great way to model this for colleagues. There are many blogging platforms available to use: Blogger, Wordpress, and Edublogs are three of the most popular. The setup is very quick and easy; all three platforms have user interfaces that are user-friendly and have lots of features. Parents can subscribe to a blog to receive posts sent to their inbox, or they can use an aggregator site such as Feedly. Just as teachers typically send home a weekly newsletter, an administrator could create a weekly blog post to share things happening at school, kudos to students and teachers, and pictures of school events.

Twitter

How do I post anything on Twitter that is valuable? I'm limited to only 140 characters! Ah, but having to be that brief and to the point, along with easily being able to share updates and pictures directly from your phone, are reasons that administrators love using Twitter as a communication tool. Twitter has become one of the most popular tools for district and school leaders to use to communicate to parents and students. We have superintendents announcing snow days via Twitter, principals sharing student work via Twitter, and teachers sending out reminders via Twitter. What a great way to communicate and share the great things happening in your district or school!

COLLABORATION

Google Apps for Education

Google has taken education by storm in the last few years with its suite of productivity, collaboration, and communication tools. At the heart of the Google Apps suite we have Gmail, Google Calendar, Google Drive, and Google Sites. These are the big four that everyone from Ivy League universities to the smallest K–12 school districts is adopting for staff and students to use. If we look at Google Apps for Education through the lens of collaboration, this is an extremely valuable tool for a digitally enhanced leader to employ. I've worked with school leaders who are looking to increase digital collaboration amongst staff and have used Google Drive to make this happen. For example, we have had administrators do this for PLC collaboration time. One person in each grade level creates a folder, shares it with the team and the administrator, and places all collaborative documents each week inside it. This keeps everything organized in one place not only for the teachers, but the principal has immediate access to the information and can provide electronic feedback when it is convenient.

Leaders can use Google Forms to collect data and information from parents, students, and staff and easily collaborate on and publish documents, spreadsheets, and presentations too.

CURATION

We have information in enormous quantity at our fingertips. What do I do with it to keep it organized and easy to recall later? Another skill for a digitally enhanced leader to employ is being able to effectively and efficiently curate content from the web. There are many web tools available that allow us to capture these pieces of information, create our own organizational scheme to place it in, and make it easy for us to share it with others from these platforms as well.

Diigo

Diigo continues to be my favorite. It is the place where I started organizing all of the great ideas and resources I come across from searching the web and from my personalized learning network (PLN). After you create your account, I'd highly recommend installing the Diigo extension for Chrome. When you come across something you'd like to save in Diigo, you click the Chrome extension, type in the tag(s) (keywords) you'd like to use to organize it, and click save. That's it. Sure, there are other bells and whistles available, but at its core, that's what Diigo does—it let's you create your own organizational scheme so you can quickly recall information you need later. For example, one of the tags I created early on is "googleforms." I like to make my tags as all one word, and anything related to using Google Forms I save with that tag attached to it. So if two weeks later I need to look it up, I just have to search by my "googleforms" tag, and I get everything I saved and tagged with that keyword.

Remember, I said the sharing piece was important too. So if you asked me to share all those resources with you, when I search on a particular tag in my Diigo library, it has its own unique link, so all I'd have to do is send you this:

https://www.diigo.com/user/kylepace/googleforms

Then you have all my resources on using Google Forms! That's handy and a great way to share with colleagues!

CREATIVITY

In my opinion, no matter what the purpose of the tool is, if we're using it to create rather than just consume, it's a good thing. Here are some tools that are great for producing new ways to share information and ideas.

Canva

Canva is a web application for creating visually appealing images. One of the things I enjoy most about Canva is that they're very much invested in teaching users how to create professional looking content. Canva can be used to create a poster,

> If we're using a tool to create rather than just consume, it's a good thing.

a logo, or an image to use in a document or a presentation. You get a lot of creative choices to pick from for free.

Powtoon

If you're looking for a really fun presentation platform then you should definitely check out Powtoon. You are no doubt familiar with presentation tools, but the features of this one definitely will not be familiar. You have loads of fun features at your disposal that give you lots of creative freedom when creating presentations to share with parents and staff.

YouTube

Yes, you can also be a star on YouTube! Ok, so maybe not a star, but video is definitely a medium to reach district and school stakeholders. Have you ever thought about creating a school YouTube channel to create and publish video messages to? Or perhaps having a Hangout On Air with a guest speaker that students and parents can watch later? This is just the beginning of the kinds of things you could publish to a schoolwide YouTube channel.

There are a lot of options that have been shared here, but don't let it overwhelm you. Pick one thing in one area to focus on, and get really good at it. Don't feel like you have to be using all of this at the same time; in fact, I'd strongly suggest you don't do that! The idea is to keep moving forward—not seeing how much or how fast you can move forward; the point is to grow and move yourself forward.

Our schools and school districts need leaders who are digitally equipped not only to help us do our jobs better, but to model appropriate use of digital media for our students and the greater community.

Three Take-Aways

1. Focus just on one of those four Cs to begin with: communication, collaboration, curation, or creativity. Hone your skills on one—don't feel like you have to begin implementing everything tomorrow!

2. Commit to one new way of sharing information based on one of the resources shared in this chapter.

3. Reflection and sharing are huge components of the success of a new endeavor. Make time to do both!

CHAPTER 3

Empowered Professional Learning

Kristen Swanson

THE NEED FOR EMPOWERED PROFESSIONAL LEARNING

Our world is changing . . . *fast*. Some generally describe these changes as the growth of the knowledge economy. In the knowledge economy, jobs require thinking, problem solving, and empathy. Jobs that don't demand higher order skills are quickly becoming scarce, making the need to think critically and connect with others more important than ever (OECD, 1996).

Schools must urgently respond to these changes in the world and the workforce. Importantly, the learning revolution must begin with us. Research shows that educators must successfully participate in connected and empowered learning experiences before they can generate similar learning experiences for students (Beglau et al., 2011). It is time to learn from others, try out new strategies, and experiment locally.

However, you may not find many examples of empowered professional learning in your district. This is not unusual. "How People Learn," one of the most widely respected white papers on effective educational practice, laments, "Many approaches to teaching adults consistently violate principles for optimal learning" (Bransford, Brown, Cocking, Donovan, & Pelligrino, 2000). Further, most educators and educational leaders deem professional learning "totally useless" (Darling-Hammond, Chung Wei, Andree, & Richardson, 2009). In fact, only 10% of educators successfully transfer new skills back to the classroom after they have attended workshops (Bush, 1984), and the one-time workshop is the most prevalent model of skills training today for educators (Yoon, Duncan, Lee, Scarloss, & Shapley, 2007).

We cannot wait for our existing systems to catch up. Instead, we must take responsibility for our own professional learning *now*.

Used with permission of Tom Murray.

RECLAIMING YOUR
PROFESSIONAL LEARNING

Ownership and empowerment go hand in hand. When we have control over our learning, it becomes impactful and effective (Pink, 2011). Today's digital age gives us opportunities to regain control of our professional learning as never before. The advent of the Internet has created an environment where content and connections are abundant. We can connect to others (and their ideas) more easily now than ever before. This creates a unique opportunity to learn in new, different ways that often transcend high price tags, traditional experts, or regional isolation. Many educators all over the world are flocking to online spaces to fill the gaps in their professional learning.

OPERATIONALIZING THE
PROCESS: THREE PHASES
FOR EMPOWERED LEARNING

While everyone's learning journey is unique, both action research and vetted educational studies reveal that there are three general phases in the process:

- curation
- reflection
- contribution

> We must take responsibility for our professional learning *now.*

It's very common for these phases to overlap and occur in a non-linear fashion. However, describing each phase in its entirety is a great place to start!

Curation

Curation is defined as the careful collection of relevant resources. While there has been curation since long before the advent of the

Internet, the web provides a wealth of new tools that can super-charge your curation skills. These tools allow you to broaden the materials to which you have access. The hardest part of curation is determining what is worth your time!

How to Curate: Three Easy Steps

Step 1: Identify the right sources to mine for helpful tools and information.

Examples include the blogs of other educators, online research journals, and Google scholar. Check out the Teach 100 (http://teach.com/teach100) for some of the top-rated blogs and resources sources in education. Edutopia (www.edutopia.org) and Connected Principals (http://connectedprincipals.com/) are also great places to find information.

Step 2: Figure out a way to have content from these sources delivered to you.

There are many different tools and devices that can deliver new content from blogs directly to *you!* They include feed readers and free apps that work on any device. See below for examples, links, and ideas.

Step 3: Tag/favorite/save things you want to use later.

Use a tool to tag and organize all of your resources. Think of this as your own, personal, digital filing cabinet. This will allow you to revisit your learning and implement the ideas you've found! When tagging, try to use a uniform tagging system. It will help you find things later on!

Top 5 Curation Tools

When curating, the right tools can make a big difference. Here are the top five free tools to support your curation.

Feedly (https://feedly.com) Feedly is a website where you can save all of your blogs, read them, and tag them. It's a one-stop shop for curation.

Flipboard (https://about.flipboard.com/) Flipboard is a great tool that makes your favorite blogs, tweets, and websites into a beautiful magazine. You can also star or save articles.

Pinterest (www.pinterest.com) Pinterest is a visual curation tool with a vibrant teacher community on it. When you see things you like (either on the web or on someone else's board) you pin it to your boards. It's simple and highly addictive!

Evernote (www.evernote.com) Evernote is a curation tool that allows you to capture, tag, and search anything you find on the web. You can also share everything you find with others in a single click.

Diigo (www.diigo.com/) Diigo is a social bookmarking tool. You save and tag things you like. You can also share your tags with others.

Reflection

Reflection is usually the second phase of the empowered learning process, and it requires the learner to assimilate new learning into existing mental schema. This can be accomplished in many ways, including collegial conversations and blogging. When it comes to reflection, the final product is less important than the process. However, reflecting in public, digital spaces allows you to get feedback from your colleagues all over the globe.

How to Reflect: Three Easy Steps

Step 1: Choose something new to try.

Once you start curating new resources, it's likely that you'll find lots of new ideas and strategies to try. Start small and choose one idea.

Step 2: Try the new idea or strategy.

Just do it, folks! Implement the strategy in your classroom.

Step 3: Tell someone else how it went. Get lots of feedback.

After you try something new, share the experience with someone. This might be through writing in a journal, having a collegial conversation, or writing a blog post. Again, the format is much less important than the process here!

Top 5 Reflection Tools

The good old fashioned sticky note—As you try things in the moment, jot down your impressions or reactions.

Coffee—Reflection with a colleague over coffee often provides valuable insight and helps you better understand the outcomes of your experiments.

A journal or notebook—Keeping your reflections in a single place can help you to reflect and document your progress over time. Teaching is challenging, and being able to see your practice transform over time is important!

Blogging tools such as Blogger (www.blogger.com) or KidBlogs (www.kidblog.org) can provide you with a digital diary for reflection. These tools are free to use and they allow you to share your reflections with the world.

Twitter (www.twitter.com), a microblogging platform, allows you to publish short reflections and images right from your phone or computer. Many teachers are using this tool for reflection, and vibrant communities of educators have sprung up in this space.

Contribution

After consuming and reflecting on new information, it's important to contribute to the learning network at large. In short, you must support the learning of others. Not only does this phase help the cycle to continue for all learners, but it also provides an active component to the learning process. Without active application and contribution, you are much less likely to internalize and transfer your learning.

How to Contribute: Three Easy Steps

Step 1: Identify existing communities of learning in your area.

Check out the learning communities that exist in your local area and online. You may already have learning communities in your district. You can also check out the local ISTE or ASCD affiliates in your state (e.g., Pennsylvania Association for Educational Communications and Technology, Michigan Computers Users in Learning, etc.). It's likely that there is also an Edcamp event near you. Find the list of upcoming events here: http://edcamp.wikispaces.com

Step 2: Try out several different communities.

Participate in several different communities, both face-to-face and virtual, to determine what meets your needs. Some people thrive in online Twitter chats, and others prefer face-to-face Edcamp events or teacher meet ups. See what works for you!

Step 3: Determine what you enjoy, and give back!

After you've experimented with several different communities, choose one that works well for you. Then, find a way to give back to that community in some way. It could be by running your own Edcamp event, or creating a space for educators to share, or posting an artifact you created in an online forum. Just keep the learning going!

Top 5 Contribution Tools

Edcamp events (http://edcamp.wikispaces.com—The Edcamp site has everything you need to know to find an Edcamp near you. These events are free and often local. Attending an Edcamp is a great way to contribute your learning.

List of ISTE affiliates (www.iste.org/lead/affiliate-directory)—This list of ISTE affiliates can help you locate a community around connected learning in your state or region.

List of synchronous Twitter chats (https://docs.google .com/spreadsheet/ccc?key=0AiftIdjCeWSXdDRLRzNsVk tUUGJpRWJhdUlWLS1Genc#gid=0)—If you prefer online communities, synchronous Twitter chats can be a great way to contribute. You can learn more about Twitter chats in Chapter 8.

National School Reform Faculty Protocols (www.nsrfhar mony.org/free-resources/protocols/a-z)—These protocols can be great tools for running or moderating a professional learning group in your school or district.

Classroom 2.0 (www.classroom20.com/)—This is a virtual community of educators that provides many opportunities for sharing, giving back, and learning.

THINKING BIG BUT STARTING SMALL

Becoming an empowered professional learner is an ongoing journey. As you begin to think about your curation-reflection-contribution cycles, remember that you're learning in a new, flexible way. Share your ideas broadly and often. Most important, remember that the change in learning must start with us!

Three Take-Aways

1. Curate to find the most relevant resources for you using tools like Feedly and Flipboard.

2. Reflect on your learning with colleagues or using online tools.

3. Give back to your learning community by checking out an Edcamp or other gathering of local educators.

REFERENCES

Beglau, M., Craig-Hare, J., Foltos, L., Gann, K., James, J., Jobe, H., Knight, J., & Smith, B. (2011). *Technology, coaching, and community: Power partners for improved professional development in primary and secondary education* (ISTE White Paper). Retrieved from www.iste.org/about/media-rela tions/2011/06/29/new-white-paper-new-standards-for-technology-coaching-debut-at-iste-2011

Bransford, J. D., Brown, A. L., Cocking, R. R., Donovan, M. S., & Pelligrino, J. W. (2000). *How people learn: Brain, mind, experience, and school.* Washington, DC: National Academies Press.

Bush, R. N. (1984). *Effective staff development in making schools more effective: Proceedings of three state conferences.* San Francisco, CA: Far West Laboratory.

Darling-Hammond, L., Chung Wei, R., Andree, A., & Richardson, N. (2009). *Professional learning in the learning profession. A status report on teacher development in the United States and abroad.* Oxford, OH: National Staff Development Council.

Organisation for Economic Co-operation and Development. (1996). *The knowledge based economy.* Paris, France: OECD. Retrieved from http://www.oecd.org/sti/sci-tech/1913021.pdf

Pink, D. (2011). *Drive.* New York, NY: Riverhead Books.

Yoon, K. S., Duncan, T., Lee, S. W. Y., Scarloss, B., & Shapley, K. L. (2007). *Reviewing* the evidence on how professional development affects student achievement. (Rep. No. 033). Washington, DC: Institute for Education Sciences, National Center for Evaluation and Regional Assistance.

CHAPTER 4

Authentic Learning

Steven Anderson @web20classroom

In the last several years, a major shift in instruction began to happen. Instead of students having access to handheld technology (tablet, laptop, etc.) only part of the school day, more and more students began to have access whenever they needed it. Either 1:1 or Bring Your Own Device (BYOD) or some combination of the two has given students the opportunity to discover learning or create new information in a variety of ways.

As many teachers, schools, and districts will tell you, the integration of digital devices at the point of learning, and this shift in instruction, are both a blessing and a challenge. On the one hand, students now have the ability to create in ways they've never been able to before. They also have access to all known knowledge through the power of the Internet. That in itself can be a challenge for many traditional educators. Now, it isn't the teacher who is the smartest person in the room, it's the devices.

When a classroom goes 1:1 or BYOD, two inevitable questions arise from teachers:

How will I know what students are looking at on their devices?

How do I make sure they are all paying attention to me, rather than social media or games?

In my experience as a director of instructional technology for a large district in North Carolina, these were the most common questions that we faced as we shifted toward BYOD. Teachers knew the power that devices could have for learning but were skeptical as to their own abilities to keep instruction where it needed to be.

The key to ensuring that any technology is used effectively—either at the point of learning, the front of the room, or somewhere else—is to ensure that content is not only relevant to the learner but it is authentic as well. It is authentic, purposeful, and meaningful learning that will engage students with or without technology in hand.

Authentic learning means that students are given problems that relate to their lives. These are problems their schools or communities are facing, so the solutions they create are practical and meaningful. The problems tie back to curriculum always, but they provide context and meaning to content that is often abstract or meaningless.

A middle school I worked with a few years ago took on a yearlong study of the effects that land development and building construction around their school would have on their local community. They looked at everything from the social aspects of losing a part of a park, to the historical aspects of having part of their school torn down to make way for progress, to the environmental aspects, including the potential pollution of a small stream and how to mitigate it. Each student in each grade level worked on different parts of this project throughout the year, and the study culminated with several suggestions being made to the city council.

Content was presented through this problem and was made more meaningful because it was happening all around the students. They had a vested interest in learning not only the nuts and bolts of the content, but how water quality affected them, or what effects on the economy the new buildings could have locally and beyond. These were not abstract concepts in books. These were real-world problems that students could relate to.

Some educators might recognize this engagement method as problem-based learning (PBL). Problem- or project-based learning has been around much longer than any device or technology. Its definition differs everywhere you go, but in essence students are given a problem and options for presenting their solution and their understanding of the curricular content that makes up that solution. This was the method we used in our district, as many of the teachers were formally trained in PBL; however, we put our efforts into creating authentic learning.

In some ways the middle school lesson I saw was PBL. There were multiple problems students were solving, and each problem had multiple different answers. But unlike the projects of traditional PBL, the middle school project was authentic. Many times traditional PBL has students take on a role they can't relate to. Students are asked to become a doctor/paleontologist/forensic scientist, all in an effort to both make the lesson/content seem interesting and also to expose students to potential career paths. What I found was that when students are working on a problem that directly affects them or their community, they become highly engaged in the learning process and want to find a solution.

SO, WHERE CAN YOU START?

You can start with simply asking students what problems they'd like to solve. Have them investigate and brainstorm what is happening in their school and community that they'd like to dive deep into. Perhaps it's a school policy they don't agree with, or maybe it's something happening in the community. Either way, students have a voice in the process. They own the learning, and that is key to authentic learning.

When students are working on a problem that directly affects them or their community, they become highly engaged in the learning process and want to find a solution.

The Buck Institute for Education is regarded as the leading source for anything and everything associated with PBL. What I really like about the resources here is that they are easy to access and highly authentic. Not only do they have a huge archive of curriculum resources, they also have videos, webinars, and more. This is a site you will spend a lot of time with whether you are new to PBL or experienced with it.

On her website (www.schrockguide.net/authentic-learning.html), Kathy Schrock has curated a large collection of resources for authentic learning. From frameworks to assessments and more, you will find a lot of great content here.

As you can probably guess, this method of learning isn't dependent on technology. Many of our teachers were trained knowing that they would gradually ease into BYOD. However, technology does enhance this type of learning. It provides students with more access to real-time information, as well as the ability to connect to more resources and create the information needed to make an argument. There's a deeper level of engagement you can't get offline.

If you are in a classroom or school that is moving more toward mobile devices for learning, it's important to know that your pedagogy has to change. Simply using devices to look up answers or take assessments isn't anything that could be done without them. Look for ways to use the devices for learning that wouldn't be possible without them, and, with your students, find truly authentic ways to deliver and master content and engage them fully.

Three Take-Aways

1. Consider an examination of school culture. How do teachers perceive student-centered learning? To what extent do students currently have choice in what and how they learn?

2. Challenge your team/school to start small. What problem is your community currently facing? Perhaps there is an issue at school that students could research and weigh in on. Or is there something that they could have impact on in the community? Start there and allow students to explore the problem and formulate their own solutions.

3. To immerse teachers in the authentic learning environments, create a professional development session that puts the learning back in the hands of educators. Consider adapting the authentic learning frameworks to your current model of professional learning to reinforce the need for learners to be deeply involved in their learning.

Blogging

George Couros @gcouros

I write to understand as much as to be understood.

—Elie Wiesel

B logging has been something that has been utilized in classrooms across the world, but only sparingly. Often, creating and maintaining a blog has been something that has been done in individual classes, as opposed to something that is common practice, no matter the teacher, throughout the school. It is a great way for learners not only to showcase their learning, but to openly reflect to an authentic audience. Although it can be daunting for schools and is not something every student is comfortable with, there are so many benefits to blogging that educators and schools need to pay more attention to it and look for meaningful ways to use it. To say there is one single benefit of blogging would be an understatement, as it offers opportunities for open reflection and collaboration, as well as for developing varying forms of literacy.

THE POWER OF OPEN REFLECTION

Several years ago, when I was a principal, I wanted to develop an understanding of how blogging would benefit students, so I started a blog of my own just to learn the technical aspects of how to create and maintain an online space. Little did I know the impact it would have on my own learning.

The process of open reflection was crucial to my own development as a learner. Clive Thompson, in his 2013 article titled "Why Even the Worst Bloggers Are Making Us Smarter," shared this same sentiment. He goes on to state that "it is easy to win an argument inside your head, but when you write for an audience, you have to be truly convincing."

As a school administrator, this act of open reflection actually made me think deeper about our work and be more proactive through this process. I knew that for any initiative in our school that I shared on my blog, I would want to really refine my thought process before I shared it with the entire world. When students blog and are sharing their learning with the whole world, they are more likely to be thoughtful than when they are sharing only with their teacher or a few peers. I have watched this effect on teachers writing their first blog post and seen how deeply they think about what they share because the whole world can see it. Yet they have no issues writing an e-mail to a colleague. The impact of an audience can actually help us improve our writing.

GLOBAL COLLABORATION

Open reflection is crucial to the process of blogging not only because the entire world can read blog posts but also because the entire world can write back. When I started off as a principal, I felt extremely isolated in my position, since there is only one principal in each school. When I started to blog, I felt that I had tapped into a community of people who were in many of the same situations I was in, but they addressed them from different experiences and perspectives. Their real-time, global feedback was extremely beneficial to my learning and made real-world connections to the work that I was doing.

What is powerful about blogging is that you don't necessarily have to find an audience; the audience usually finds you. There are blogs written by librarians, kindergarten teachers, science teachers, superintendents, and basically everyone in between. An audience does not have to consist of thousands of people but only a small number to make a difference. It is not about connecting with everyone but finding your "tribe."

Students obviously can see the same benefit of connecting with an authentic audience. When Martha Payne, a nine-year-old (at the time) student from Scotland, started her blog about school lunches (located at http://neverseconds.blogspot.com/), I am sure that no one had any idea of the impact that it would make. At first, Martha realized that her dad could see it and highlighted that in her first post saying, "The good thing about this blog is Dad understands why I am hungry when I get home." Quickly, her blog gained national and international attention, from people such as Jamie Oliver and others from all over the world. According to the Wikipedia post about her blog (at nine years old she had a Wikipedia post written about her!), she not only helped change the choices of food in the cafeteria (they were given unlimited amounts of fruits, vegetables, and bread), but in less than two months, she had ended up raising over £90,000 for "Mary's Meals," which was used to build a new kitchen for a primary school in Blantyre, Malawi. There is more to the story, but as Shelley Wright has been quoted as saying, "Kids often defy expectations, if you give them the opportunity."

WHAT YOU MODEL IS WHAT YOU GET

Although many could say that Martha's story is not the norm with blogging (either by adults or students), it is essential to realize that we live in a world where everyone can have a voice, and we need to empower our students to make a change. If we are going to do this successfully, though, educators need to first jump in themselves. Simple tasks for bloggers, such as categorizing and tagging posts, become ways not only to make content easily searchable for both readers and authors, but also for authors to identify key ideas. This process benefits teachers in teaching the technical aspects of writing a blog and also helps them understand the power of sharing through the medium for deep learning and reflection. In Dean Shareski's article on "How to Make Better Teachers" (2010), he states his belief that teachers who have really put a focus on their own blogging have not only improved their learning but have also improved the learning of others:

> If you look at the promise of Professional Learning Communities that our schools have invested thousands, more likely millions to achieve, blogs accomplish much of the same things. The basic idea of the PLC is to have teachers share practice/data and work in teams to make improvements. A good blog does this and more. While the data may not be school specific, great bloggers know how to share data and experience that is both relevant and universal so any reader can contribute and create discussion.

Kelli Holden, a teacher in Parkland School Division in Alberta, Canada, is a great example of how blogging can not only make an impact on one's learning, but ultimately on the learning of one's students. Her blog, "Mrs. Holden's Blog" (www.psdblogs.ca/kholden) is a great mix of her professional learning and stories from her classroom. Her willingness to write this blog has had an impact on her students.

Maddisyn, a fourth-grade student in Kelli Holden's class, shared a post on the Parkland School Division blog "184 Days of Learning" (a collaborative blog that answers the question, "What did you learn today?" every single day of the school year), sharing her enthusiasm for viewing a "livestream" with author Peter H. Reynolds and her thoughts on "making her mark." Not only did Maddisyn write down her thoughts, but she added a piece of her artwork to accentuate the post. Less than 12 hours after she posted on the blog, Peter H. Reynolds commented to Maddisyn, complimented her on her artwork, and encouraged her to continue to make her "mark" in the world. Not only did Maddisyn learn that she had a voice, but she learned it could reach anyone, including the author. If it weren't for Holden's willingness to blog and share that learning with her students, I am not sure Maddisyn (and so many of Holden's other students) would have had this opportunity. There is a huge opportunity in sharing work you are passionate about with an authentic audience. Teachers need to find ways to create these opportunities.

FINAL THOUGHTS

Blogging has been around for a while now, and as long as people have something to say, it will be a part of our lives. The power of the platform is that you are not limited to writing; it is conducive also to many other, different aspects of literacy. You can make a video, share a podcast, create a visual, or write, all while connecting with an audience that wants not only to learn from the blogger, but alongside the blogger. If we are going to be successful with this type of initiative, we will have to adopt a culture where everyone is a teacher, and everyone is a learner, and develop this practice not only for our students but also for our own professional learning. If we are open to learning and sharing with one another, in the end, we can only become better for our students.

Three Take-Aways

1. Find three educator blogs to read and get ideas from. Two bloggers I suggest are Pernille Ripp (pernillesripp.com) and John Spencer (www.spencerideas.org).

2. Start your own blog. Sites I would suggest to start are blogger.com, wordpress.com, and edublogs.org.

3. Write a reflection once a week. Ask yourself, "What did I learn this week?" and write it in your blog. Write for yourself, but know the world can read it. If you make this a priority, it will make a difference.

REFERENCES

Shareski, D. (2010, November 16). How to make better teachers. *Huffington Post Education*. Retrieved from http://www.huffingtonpost.com/dean-shareski/how-to-make-better-teache_b_783392.html

Thompson, C. (2013, August 17). Why even the worst bloggers are making us smarter. *Wired*. Retrieved from http://www.wired.com/2013/09/how-successful-networks-nurture-good-ideas-2/

CHAPTER

6

Giving Our Students a Voice Through Global Connections

Shannon Miller @shannonmmiller

As you walk into the classroom, you see 45 excited kindergarteners, two teachers, and the teacher librarian gathered on the floor around the screen in the front of the room. They are talking about the Iowa animal PBL (project-based learning) project they are kicking off and waiting for a special guest to arrive on Skype.

Skype rings, and it is children's author Seymour Simon. The kids all wave and greet him like they are seeing an old friend. To them, Mr. Simon is another beloved teacher.

One little boy raises his hand to say, "I loved when you read the eBook about planets to us. I am happy to see you again." Seymour smiles ear to ear. He feels the same way and has gotten to know the students in our school throughout the year.

We explain to the children that he is going to help them create the driving questions for their Iowa animal PBL projects. They come up to the laptop in the front of the classroom one at a time. Seymour and each student talk about research, writing, the student's Iowa animal, and what the student would like to create to show learning.

Six weeks pass, and in the Iowa Animal Project Parade, kindergarteners showcase the projects they created to demonstrate the answer to the driving question. Parents, teachers, and others fill the library to see their beautiful creations and hear about their learning, while Seymour Skypes in to be part of this special event too. Students will once again talk with him one by one, showing their projects and answering the driving question they created together.

Through this project and others, we created a rich learning experience for our students that transcended the four walls of the classroom by bringing in excitement, expertise, and friendship through technology, innovation, and a virtual connection. We created the dots that successfully led each and every student through the process of connecting, collaborating, and creating within a learning experience that they will never forget. We gave them a voice in their learning, and this makes all the difference within our schools, throughout education, and the world.

As I started making connections on Twitter and other social networks, I saw the potential for using Skype and similar platforms as a way to bring other students, teachers, authors, experts, and others into our school. I was no longer the only teacher librarian within my district and could virtually collaborate with others anytime and anywhere. It was very rewarding and motivating for the students, teachers, and me when we started learning with new friends in other parts of the world. We had so much to gain from these connections—and a lot to share as well.

When the eighth-grade science class had a project about space, we connected with NASA and their astronauts. When the fifth graders did an author study on Michael Buckley's books, we Skyped him in to the library to lead the discussion at the end of the unit. When my social media class wanted to study gaming and create a game of their own, we connected on Twitter and Skype with Alan Murray, the creator of Halo. When the first graders were learning how to sequence steps, we connected with the Capstone Publishing art department, and they explained how to create cookbooks and the importance of easy steps in cookbooks for children. They even Skyped into the library to cook and follow directions from one of their cookbooks with the first graders. What an exciting day that was for all of us.

Used with permission of Arturo Avina.

One of the most special connections for me was when we Skyped with my friend Art Avina-Moreno and his kindergarteners in Los Angeles. Art and I met on Twitter after he shared a video that his class created. I wanted to connect with Art and his little ones so they could share the experience with my students in Iowa. It was great fun and one of the best Skypes!

But it really meant so much more when Art wrote me later that day and said,

Hi Shannon! This may sound silly, but I've kept going back to these pictures over and over again today. It almost gives me chills that our kids connected this way. It's ironic that living in LA, the rest of the world is so closed off to my students. . . . It somewhat limits what they are exposed to. Having downtown LA in our backyard does not translate into multicultural experiences for them. They don't venture out of their neighborhood much, and their world is pretty much school and home. For them to talk to kids that [are the] "same, same but different" (pun intended) in another part of the country is groundbreaking for them.

With Skype we were able not only to hear about something really awesome other children created, but also to make a difference in their lives—just as they made a difference in ours.

You can read about our first Skype connection on my blog, "The Library Voice." You can find the link on this book's companion website: http://corwin.com/connectededucators.

© Shannon Miller

Later in the year, my son Hagan and I Skyped again with Art and his students. This time our connection happened at our home in the horse pasture. Hagan introduced them to our horse Roman and what it was like living out in the country in Iowa. It was such a special experience for all of us—and one I will never forget.

You can read more about their visit to Iowa on the companion website, http://corwin.com/connectededucators.

We live in a world that is connected through social media, broadband, and platforms that allow us to have virtual conversations. By having access to these things, we, as educators and lead learners, can take down the walls of our schools, libraries, and classrooms to connect ourselves and our school community globally. In schools around the world, we are hearing story after story of how these connections are truly changing the way learning and teaching is taking place. As you can see, by collaborating, creating, and connecting with others, we are giving our students experiences and opportunities to become more passionate about their learning.

My dear friend and author Peter Reynolds wrote a book called *The Dot* (Candlewick Press, 2003). One of my favorite lines of the book is,

> Her teacher said, "Just make a mark and see where it takes you."

Just like the kindergarteners in rural Iowa, we can give all of our young people the chance to connect with others around the world, enriching their education and lives. By using digital platforms such as Skype and Google Hangout, we are giving them the dots they will need to make these connections.

And most of all—we are giving them the voice that they will need to make their very own mark on the world.

Three Take-Aways

1. Being connected through Skype and Google Hangout is a powerful way to take your students outside of the school walls into the world. It can enhance any subject and engage your young people like never before.

2. Through Skype, Twitter, and other digital tools, you can give your students a global voice and a passion for being connected. With these social networks and digital tools, you can bring authors, illustrators, publishers, experts, and others into your libraries, classrooms, and school communities.

3. We have so much to bring to each other through Skype and other tools for connecting. Always think *big* and outside of the box when creating these connections. The sky is the limit. And don't forget what you have to bring to others as well.

Student Personal Learning Networks

Lisa Nielsen @InnovativeEducator

E ducators are creating their own sources for learning via personal learning networks (PLNs). These are the connections individual learners make on platforms like Twitter, Facebook, Google Communities, Instagram, blogs, and more to suit their specific learning needs.

PLNs provide a great means for any educator to join global communities around an area of interest. They provide access to the insight and ideas of other practitioners, leaders, and experts in a way that just wasn't possible before this explosion of interactivity.

PLNs have become popular with educators, because they provide professional learning opportunities and support in a selected area of interest anytime, anywhere. They have become an important method lead learners use to find what new knowledge is most relevant to them, and to become in turn more relevant in their chosen career specialty.

Like their teachers, students are also seeking new, relevant, and usable knowledge. Like educators, they want to make connections in their areas of interest. Educators who "get it" are able to use their expertise to help students develop their own network of go-to idea leaders.

Of course, many students are already doing this. Many are connected and reaching out using these tools. With the guidance and support of caring, knowledgeable, and trusted adults, student PLNs can have more depth and more power.

This chapter provides a five-step process that will help all educators become key partners to students seeking to develop and grow their personal learning networks.

1. CONTEMPLATE

Students will need to reflect on what they want to accomplish when they begin to build a learning network. Teachers can guide them by asking them to think about important questions such as these:

- What are you passionate about?
- Is there something that breaks your heart?
- What troubles you?
- Is there something you love and want to know more about?
- Do you want to spread the word about a great idea, music group, cause, or problem?

These questions lay out the basis of the network they will create. Second-grade teacher Courtney Woods knows this firsthand.

Mrs. Woods's class was troubled when they discovered that their community had a drop in tourism. They felt that if only more people knew how great their city of Bathurst, Canada, was, tourism would increase. As a result, they made a panoramic picture using Photosynth that explained the popular attractions in their town.

That was Step 1, but what they hoped to accomplish was getting the word out to those key stakeholders who could increase tourism. They had to consider who they should reach out to, which brings us to the next step.

2. CONSIDER

Students will have two considerations: audience and medium.

First, they'll need to consider who to target. Who will help them best grapple with what they are contemplating?

Second, they'll need to consider what medium is best to communicate their message. This might mean commenting on a blog, sending out tweets, starting a Facebook page, or joining a Google Community. Help your students explore and determine which platform makes the most sense.

This article, written by a high school student, might be a useful one to consider some of the ways social media hashtags are being used: "Hashtag Activism Is Here to Stay," by Avi Sholkoff. You can find the link on this book's companion website: http://corwin.com/connectededucators.

Once students consider their audience and the platform they'll use, they are ready for the next step.

3. CONSUME

Students should consume information from various outlets, before they step forward. This will give them the lay of the land and a feel for how things work. Some people call this *lurking*.

Give students some focus areas to think about as they are doing this.

- What content do they think is favorable?
- What content gets the most engagement?

- Do those contributing use a shorthand, or do they write with proper grammar?
- What is not effective?

Rather than asking about traditional current events, ask students to collect real stories of people using their network to address a problem. Have students share these stories, and discuss what they notice. Let the successes of others help inform what your students will do.

If you're looking for an example to share with your students, check out the tweets Mrs. Woods's class sent to the key people whom they wanted to know about their project. These were the people they felt could help them spread their town's Photosynth more widely. They shared their work with the hosts of their favorite talk show as well as the local tourism bureau. They also wanted the minister of education to see the kind of work second graders could do, and they thought the creators of Photosynth might appreciate hearing about how they were using their product too.

And why stop there? Bill Gates was the creator of the Windows 8 platform they were using, so they tweeted to him too. You can see their original Tweets by searching "Twitter in Second Grade" at http://innovativeeducator.com.

4. CONNECT

Connecting with others is crucial to building a learning network. Once you've helped students contemplate *what* they want to communicate, and consider *who* it is they want to communicate with and *how,* they are ready to connect!

This is where the message is *oh so important* and the guidance of a connected educator is key.

Will your students be building their network by commenting on blogs?

If so, visit Mrs. Yollis's classroom blog. (You'll find the URL on this book's companion website: http://corwin.com/connectededucators.) There you'll learn about writing a one-point comment that doesn't add very much to the post, and a two-point comment that adds something new to the conversation. You'll also learn about the anatomy of a comment, which includes things like having a topic sentence and a closing sentence (to give readers an insight into why you are participating) supported by details.

Maybe your students have decided to build their network using Twitter. If so, you'll want to show them how they can search a hashtag representing their interest, and then select "People" so they can connect with others who are passionate about that topic.

Instagram was the tool of choice for high school student Alex Laubscher. Alex developed an extensive network with others who share his love for zine culture and illustrating. Alex's network helped him learn how to produce and sell his self-created zines. Alex posts his work on Instagram and comments on the work of others. He has since grown a tight-knit following consisting of hundreds of others who appreciate his work. Read more about how Alex built his network by searching "Alex" at http://innovativeeducator.com.

Alex was also able to meet the faces behind the minds he met online, which brings us to our final step.

5. CONVENE

Today students are fortunate: They are no longer tied down by geography when it comes to finding others who share their interests. They can easily make global connections using the right hashtag and/or knowing how to find others online who share an interest. While it is fantastic to meet people online from around the world, when possible, find ways to convene face to face. This is a powerful way to strengthen those connections.

Google educator groups and edcamps have popped up around the globe to bring like-minded folks together in person. Meetups are ways to "find your people" and meet up with others who share your interests. And, then of course there are professional organizations that bring people together.

This is how Alex Laubscher met members of his learning network. The Society of Illustrators brings together illustrators at a variety of gatherings and events. Alex attended one of their largest events of the year, MoCCA Fest, which is an art festival that brings illustrators together in one place. In attendance were many members of Alex's learning network. He was finally able to meet the faces behind the minds he had begun to know so well.

Regardless of whether adults are aware or directly involved, meeting strangers on the Internet is no longer taboo. It is a part of growing your learning network. This is where another important role for educators emerges. Help students make these connections safely and responsibly, just like we do in face-to-face interactions with people in our community.

For young students, this might mean supervised visits with a chaperone present.

High school student Nikhil Goyal turned to his extensive learning network for input and guidance when he wrote the book, *One Size Does Not Fit All* (Bravura Books, 2012). Nikhil met numerous members of his learning network face to face. He gives this advice: "I would suggest trying to meet people in your PLN in a public place: a coffee shop, restaurant, bookstore, etc." As a high school student, he also had set times to check in with his parents.

Being safe also means knowing how to check digital footprints to ensure the people you are meeting are who they say they are, and that they are people whom you would like to add to your network. Alex explains it this way: "My advice is that you should use your head and common sense. There are ways to know if it's right to meet someone and there are safe ways to do it."

Jabreel Chisley, a student blogger covering topics of social justice and educational equality, reflects on his experience meeting others around the nation who share his passion: "I knew it was safe because everyone in my PLN had a verifiable background and they were all consistent."

If you're wondering what happened with the tweets Mrs. Woods's class sent out, nearly everyone they tweeted (and more!) responded. In the end, the tourism bureau shared their great work on the bureau's Facebook page, and there was a good deal of convening. The class got a face-to-face visit from the hosts of their favorite show, and Bill Gates invited Mrs. Woods to meet members of her learning network face to face during Microsoft's Partners in Learning Global Summit in Prague.

CONCLUSION

In today's world, what you know has much less value than who you know and how to make the most of those connections. That is why it is so important to support students in building a robust learning network.

Zak Malamed explains the importance of this work. Zak is the founder of the nonprofit Student Voice (StuVoice.org) and the hashtag #StuVoice. He brings together those passionate about the topic of student voice online via Twitter chats, Google Hangouts, Facebook, and more. He also brings these people face-to-face once a year at Student Voice Live Summit. "It is the responsibility of our community and more specifically, that of our schools to not only teach students how to be safe online, but also about how to use the Internet to their advantage," Zak shares. "This is an essential skill in a 21st Century society and we can best learn how to teach students and each other through experiencing ourselves how people are utilizing the Internet."

Whether you are working in an elementary classroom like Mrs. Woods or Mrs. Yollis, or working with teens like Alex, Nikhil, or Zak, you need to understand and support the development of powerful learning networks that will assist your students in becoming contributors to society.

Three Take-Aways

1. **Start collecting:** Keep your eye out for stories of people or movements that have succeeded because of the power of their networks. These examples will inspire you and your students.

2. **Explain your journey:** Consider making a presentation that focuses on how you achieved success as you moved through each of the five steps (contemplate, consider, consume, connect, convene) and that provides some outcomes as well.

3. **Take action:** Courtney Woods's second-grade class used the power of the PLN to increase tourism in their community. Talk to your students about ways in which they can develop a PLN to make a difference in yours. The work that results will be an experience they won't forget.

CHAPTER 8

Digital Learning Tools

Adam Bellow @Adambellow

We live in and teach in a truly remarkable time. In the last 20 years, technological advances have made it possible to bring all the information in the world to our fingertips in ways we only dreamed about a short time ago. I am sure I am not alone in saying that I remember waiting to go to the library to research information in order to quench my thirst for knowledge or complete some mandatory assignment. Today, whether you are a classroom educator or an administrator, you need only ask Google, Siri, Cortana, and so on, and the answer comes right to you in an instant.

For educators, the easy access to all the world's information can be both amazing and sometimes daunting, especially if you were teaching "BG" (Before Google). I remember the first time a student asked a question in my classroom that I didn't know the answer to right away. While I apologized for not knowing the information off the top of my head and explained to the student that I would have to look it up later, one of his peers got out a phone and had the answer for the class almost instantly. My classroom was never the same again. And neither was the role of the teacher in my eyes. The connected world can be a bit disconcerting, but in some ways be very transformative and even freeing.

Today it is not just the access to seemingly unlimited information that has changed the classroom, it is the growing number of tools we and our students have access to using in order to deepen our engagement, understanding, and potential for teaching, learning, and sharing.

Utilizing new technologies, especially digital tools, can sometimes feel like a complex or overwhelming process.

THE LIST OF PROS SOMETIMES MIMICS THE CONS

- New tools pop up almost all the time.
- The tools usually iterate very quickly to stay ahead and remain relevant, which means that you might get used to something and come back to find a feature or the tool itself is gone.
- The technology platforms (phones/computers/tablets/etc.) constantly evolve, which may lead to dramatic redesigns and make the tools that were familiar to you yesterday appear foreign to you today.

So for some this list is exciting and for some terrifying—or perhaps both.

Let's make taking the first step to integrating digital tools in the classroom or into the culture of a school more manageable by answering the 5 W's and an H:

Who

That's an easy one. You're reading this book, so I will presume that you are looking for ways to become more connected and make more out of what technology has to offer in your classroom. There are digital tools out there for everyone and everything. "Knowing the who" is important though. As in, "Is this a tool for me, as an educator?" or "Is this a tool for my students to use?" A lot of education tools are focused on both, but some will be more heavily aimed at the educator user. For example, Remind (www.remind.com) is an incredible platform that allows educators to communicate with parents and students through text and app messages. While the messages are intended for students and parents, the tool itself is mostly used by the educator programming the communiqués. Not every tool will be useful in your classroom or for your set of students, but with so many to choose from, we can all build a toolbox that will benefit our specific classrooms or schools. If you are reading this and saying, "Well, I teach X and there is nothing out there for me," you need to read on and search a little harder. With more than 1,000 iPad apps dedicated to physical fitness educators, I am sure every person in a school will be able to find more than a few to choose from.

What

Oh boy—this is a challenging question, especially if you're just getting started. The answer is that there are thousands of tools. That is probably an understatement, and the sheer number of tools can be daunting. There are a few listed here in this chapter, and there are many others that I am sure you have heard of and are reading about in other chapters in this book. Plus there are lots of books on the topic, including (shameless plug) a book I cowrote with Steve Dembo called *Untangling the Web: 20 Tools to Power Up Your Teaching* (Corwin, 2013).

A good point to remember is that there are plenty of tools out there, and not every tool is for every person. So if everyone is raving about some tool and you don't see it working in your classroom, then don't fret; you'll find the one that is right for you.

People ask me all the time where I go to learn about new tools to use and share. I find tons of great tools in my Twitter feed, usually with the hashtag #Edtech attached to the tweet. I read great blogs like Richard Byrne's Free Technology for Teachers or Larry Ferlazzo's Websites of the School Day, I attend edcamps, and I generally learn of tools by talking to other connected educators there. I also learn about tools for students from students themselves. I love to look at kids' iPads or the favorites lists on their devices and see what they are finding useful or fun to work with. And just because an app wasn't created specifically for education, don't rule it out. So many apps that are not designed specifically for education, like Instagram and Voxer, can have great purpose in the classroom when a talented educator examines how they can enhance their practice. Twitter is a great example of this. Twitter was never intended to become what it has for educators, but educators see its value and have become some of the most fervent users and adopters.

Your list of great tools will likely be different from your colleagues' lists in some or even many ways—and that is fine. I strongly suggest openly sharing what you find with colleagues. It is a great way to start a dialogue that will likely lead to finding more tools as well as interesting ways to use them in your classroom. A recommendation would be to even have a face-to-face share of the best digital tools or resources before any staff meetings.

Where

The beauty of most of our digital tools today is that they are web-based and accessible from anywhere. Years ago when I was working on multimedia projects with my students, they had to continue to edit their student film project on the exact same computer they began on, because the software and storage we were using was machine-based. They were tethered to that machine in order to do the work—it was quite hard and limited the amount of time they could spend on the project, which affected the overall output. Today's tools live largely in the cloud. That is to say, we can work with them and access them anywhere we have an Internet connection—school, home, a coffee shop, or even some buses and planes. By being device- and platform-agnostic, and by leveraging cloud-based storage for saving projects, tools like WeVideo make editing video something that can be done in class, at home, or even on a smartphone.

The concept of anywhere and anytime access to powerful tools is still fairly new. But as more schools and students homes' continue to get high-speed access, the where expands dramatically and allows students to learn and create from anywhere and at any time.

Why

To enhance teaching or learning. It is a simple answer, but it all boils down to this explanation.

Every once in a while there are tools that come about that don't necessarily move the pedagogical needle or bring education forward, but they will save teachers time doing a simple task or they will bring a (for lack of a more technical term) "cool factor" to the learning that wouldn't be there without the use of the tool. There are always some exceptions to the rule, but if you find yourself saying, "I am going to use technology in my classroom today" and don't really see the benefit as to what you are using, or if you feel that the way you are using it with the students won't enhance their learning, then it might be time to reevaluate it's use.

You don't need to use digital tools to replace all things in your classroom. Just because you can grade an exam via your cell phone app doesn't mean you have to do it that way.

Digital tools have come a long way in the past five years, and many of them are malleable and able to provide a platform for students to create and share in ways never before realized in the classroom. For example, I remember having publishing parties in school, which took place usually on a Friday when the children in the class had finished a piece of writing. The teacher would invite us to read our final work to the class and we would clap and have a special class snack. The work would then be "published" and stapled onto the bulletin board in the back of the room. Today we can (and should) be encouraging students to create and share with a genuine audience, as it is so easy to do and will provide real-world feedback in addition to opening up so many new avenues for connection and learning. This can be done by actually publishing the student work on a blog via KidBlog and then tweeting out the piece with the hashtag #Comments4Kids (a hashtag started by

William Chamberlain that encourages people to read and leave constructive and positive comments on student work).

This is an example of a classic tech versus nontech debate. The setting up of a blog site for each student will not be as quick as moving the students to the back of the room for a publishing party. It isn't hard by any means, but the first time you do it, it will take a few minutes. But the benefit for the students having both the real-world feedback and knowing that they are published authors in the same way that any modern author or newspaper writer is published makes the learning and the work that goes into the writing more real. It raises the stakes for them, and the fact that anyone can read their work will greatly increase the quality of the product.

Our students live in a world that offers them many more opportunities than the one that you and I grew up and went to school in. Their expectations of what is possible in class are (and should be) higher than what I considered possible in the education I received in the 1980s. The digital tools we have access to level the playing field for creators, so they can all connect with consumers. When we realize these new tools and mediums can unlock student potential and allow them to be creators of content that can have value and impact beyond our own classroom walls, we will no longer say "why," but rather "why not?"

When

When do we introduce the digital tools to the students, or when do we start using these tools for ourselves? The latter part of that is easy. You should starting playing with digital tools now. Some you can use today or tomorrow to improve what you were going to do in class. Some might be put on a list of tools that students might use for their next project.

Start now, but start slowly. You can't use and evaluate a large number of tools at the same time. You'll want to try out a tool, see if it is something that benefits you and your students, use it in the classroom, and evaluate what worked and what didn't. Tweak the use or junk it.

In short, there is no time like the present to start incorporating digital tools into your classroom to enhance the teaching and learning.

How

How can be a bit tricky. There is the technical how, as in "How do I use this tool?" which is usually solved by the tool's how-to section, which can easily be supplemented with a good tutorial on YouTube or a great blog post. (Basically, type the name of the tool and "tutorial" into Google, and you are sure to find some really helpful info).

But then there is the "How do I incorporate this tool into my practice?" Using a digital tool in the classroom is more than just saying "Today we will use X"—it is about really working the tool into the learning objective or outcome and not making the tool itself the objective.

Likely, as you look at and play with new tools, you will instantly see connection points to what you are teaching and ways that you can share this new potential with your students in order to have them connect to the content or create in a way that they haven't done before. As you explore new tools, you will work on your own evaluation system that will guide you in whether you adopt them as part of your "digital diet." Some of your criteria may have to do with issues of student data privacy and age of the users, and others may have to do with the actual usefulness versus time-to-learn quotient of the tool. Often there are great tools out there that offer a lot of functionality, but they don't fully fit the bill for the age group of the user or the time investment required to use with students. Evaluating tools is something that cannot be rubric-ized; it is an organic process, and so it is better to develop your evaluation skills over time as you expose yourself to the new tools.

"Yeah, But. . . ."

Read in Case of Emergency:

There are always the "what-ifs." Perhaps what-ifs have kept you from implementing new tools in your classroom. You can read about the most common what-ifs and a get few pieces of advice for dealing with digital tools on this book's companion website: http://corwin.com/connectededucators.

And in the end it comes down to you—the user—the teacher. You live and teach in an amazing time. And your students learn in an amazing time. Using these new tools can seem like more work at times. Sometimes things won't work the way you want. But that is true of traditional teaching methods too.

Three Take-Aways

1. **Start locally:** Talk with other educators about what tools they are using or trying out in the school or classroom. This can be a face-to-face conversation with those in your school or district, or a question posed to the #Edchat community on Twitter. That gives you a quick litmus test of what's out there and what other educators are finding useful.

2. **Sharing is caring:** Once you find and try a new tool, share it with others. One idea that I have used in the past is asking teachers and admins to share a new useful tool or tip at each faculty meeting. It is a quick, icebreaker-style way to learn something new. Plus, if you want to learn more, you can follow up after the meeting with the person who shared the tool you are interested in.

3. **Start small:** With so many tools popping up on the scene every day, it is easy both to be overwhelmed and to overwhelm others. Make a commitment to stick with a tool until you find something truly better to introduce. This way you, your students, and your fellow educators can all try the tool and become proficient at using it rather than just be subjected to it before moving to yet another tool.

CHAPTER 9

Putting the Horse Before the Cart

Contemporary Learning and Practice as Policy Drivers

Pam Moran @Pammoran

Source: Eric Patnoudes @NoApp4Pedagogy

W hy consider the impact of policy upon contemporary public education? I learned long ago from a mentor to question the role of policy as the driver of the work of educators, because too often policy making is about serving the interests of bureaucrats rather than making sense for learners. Over decades I have observed that educational policy determines how funding gets allocated, redirected, and spent. Policy circumscribes boundaries for educators and learners. Policy sets direction. And, policy limits possibilities.

As a young teacher I worked in a model middle school where an expectation to constantly push beyond horizons of traditional schooling to support all learners was designed into the culture, just as an architect designs form into a building to reflect how people plan to use it. In that school, educators became architects of learning, creating innovative approaches to schedules, physical space, time use, assessments, curricula, pedagogy, and resources. The team, both teachers and administrators, considered the functional nature of our work to educate all children to the highest levels of Bloom's taxonomy as driving the formation of local policy. This was the norm in a time when the governance of local public education by federal and state policy was still relatively limited in scope.

In my first brush with policy as a young teacher and then in graduate courses as an aspiring administrator, I learned that policy should be as broad as possible in language and scope to provide flexibility to educators to accomplish the work they are charged to do. Over four decades in education, I have watched formation of policy increasingly used to control and limit the innovative potential of public educators in the field, indeed to prescribe and standardize as much of the school day as possible. It is not unusual for me to read in blogs and tweets written by educators that exploring possibilities and trying new strategies to reach young learners can't happen because "it's against policy."

I fear this shift in mindset about policy does not well serve the many connected educators, administrators and teachers alike, who are living through one of the significant turning points in history—the rise of the global communication network. Nothing in the last 100 years has had the potential to impact education to the degree that new technologies now impact it. The rise of the Internet has fundamentally changed the world, politically, socially, economically, and educationally.

While other sectors encourage and invest in design thinking, invention, and innovation to boost the creative capital generated from employees, educational policy often has become a barrier to that occurring in our field. It hasn't always been that way. My early mentor, a creative who was ahead of his time, believed the critical functions of education should begin with questions rather than answers. He used to say, "It's easier to get forgiveness than permission." He also believed that policy should enable, not disable, educators in their work. He taught me three questions to consider as a basis for enacting policy:

- Why do we need this policy?
- What will this policy do to serve the best interests of learners?
- How might this policy create unintended consequences that actually work against learning?

I come back to those three questions and ask them of myself as policies are written, revised, and deleted in the school district where I work. I know the best intended policies often are created in response to rare events, can backfire and negatively impact the very interests of those we serve, and almost always result in unintended consequences.

In recent years, I've seen educational policies proliferate and manuals grow from one- to three-inch binders and then to webpage after webpage of PDFs of what often seems a version of rule making gone wild at the national, state, and local levels. However, whenever a rationale for new policy emerges, I ask others and myself, "How will this policy create a pathway that supports educators, students, and communities to receive the best educational services possible? Then, how will this policy protect both individuals and communities in our schools, if that is a need?"

Too often, I've found that creation of policy represents a boundary-setting response grounded in one of the following: fear, a kneejerk reaction to a negative event, or the "cult of efficiency" that rules through control and standardization rather than being a driver of changes that are in the best interests of learners and those who serve them in public schools.

From my perspective, rather than setting forward vision for the changes our learners need to support them in contemporary educational settings, policy serves more often to reflect the reductionist beliefs of people who are not students of education and who oversimplify the complexity of contemporary changes emerging from technology advances, neuroscience learning research, and cultural shifts. Whether a policy is developed to define the use of value-added teacher assessment or establish charter schools, those who research, recommend, approve, and enact policy often have no idea of its impact in classrooms.

For example, limiting use of the Internet as an educational tool kit filled with experts and expertise falls squarely into many local policies that misinterpret the scope of what the Federal Children's Internet Protection Act (CIPA) meant to control, from access to online pornography to other materials deemed harmful to minors. Should limits exist for what connected teachers and learners can access using school technologies? Absolutely. Should those limits be so exhaustive in terms of filtering by policy that the educational resource learning potential of the Internet becomes almost non-existent? Absolutely not.

The district where I work expects children to be both producers and consumers of content, inside and outside the walls of our schools. This means that local Internet use policy enables access to a wide range of experiential tools and resources available in the virtual world. Our policy falls squarely into enforcing CIPA and state law while allowing contemporary educators and learners to post and use media to pursue learning and professional development interests, engage in resourcing information and connectivity to support curricula, seek and share learning opportunities with authentic audiences, and find and learn from expert mentors. This cannot happen if policy at the local, state, or national level assumes that learners and teachers lack the capability to competently learn how to safely and purposely use Internet tools of learning, including but not limited to social media, Google scholar, books and apps, peer-reviewed research, commercial sites, and informal and formal virtual learning opportunities such as MOOCs, Twitter chats, or a back channel like TodaysMeet.

Today almost all humans participate in the global communication network. I believe our educational systems must afford young people opportunities to learn to use the scope of that network's potential for educational purposes. This will not happen by chance. Educators, parents, and students must participate in forming policies that encourage rather than limit the capability to explore uses of the global communication network as a learning tool. Otherwise, the already growing gap in technology use between formal education and the real world will accelerate in width and depth.

When policy makers respond with a "cart before the horse" policy in an urge to protect contemporary educators and learners from more than what CIPA intended to legally protect them from, it reduces our learners' capabilities to learn how to find and use credible sources, stay safe, and discover the agency within their own voices to influence and contribute to the global learning network. It doesn't matter whether it's YouTube, Twitter, or simply accessing a variety of search engines, when we, by policy, close down access today, we limit our students' potential to learn from the most important suite of educational resources that have existed in human history.

In my district we've built policy that defines the important parameters of responsible use of technology by staff and students. Students and staff occasionally push past those boundaries with behaviors we deem inappropriate. We choose to deal with those behaviors, not with the technology the transgressors used. Two decades ago, we would never have taken pencils away from all students because one student wrote a bullying note. Similarly, we have agreed today that we won't limit access to devices, "bring your own" or ours, because a student stepped over a policy boundary. We do use a robust filtering system to ensure that inappropriate content, such as that on pornography sites, is filtered. However, we do not limit the universe of access to sites such as YouTube that our students and teachers use daily in their learning.

Instead of constraining Internet access through policies based upon perspectives of people with little educational technology expertise or contemporary teaching experience in classrooms, leaders need to build policy based upon the work of education's professional explorers, who are figuring out how to safely use the Internet as an effective learning resource. This means identifying pioneering users and encouraging them to document the paths they take so they can share how they best navigate through challenges to their work with learners. We can learn from them how to develop and implement effective policy that reflects what is in the best interest of learners and learning, rather than accept constraints shaped by bureaucratic policy makers, education corporations looking to build policies that put funding in their pockets, or politicians feeding off of a society's media-induced fears.

Policy must affirm the work of those who explore the frontiers of contemporary learning and educational practice to make sense of how to form reasonable parameters that do not overconstrain the limitless learning possibilities of digital technology access. As architects of learning, we need to allow policy form to follow contemporary functions of education. In doing so, we can build a model that puts policy in its proper place.

Three Take-Aways

Before creating education policy that will drive contemporary learning decisions and practices,

1. **Convene key stakeholders:** A diverse leadership team (teachers, parents, administrators) can together consider and identify guiding principles that frame contemporary learning goals and that respond to both educational needs and legal parameters (CIPA, for example).

2. **Ask key questions.** When developing policy, the team should consider the policy's function before describing its form. Why is the policy needed? What problem will the policy solve? What unanticipated consequences might ensue from implementation? How will the policy be interpreted in its most literal sense? Is the policy both broad and narrow enough? Who will be responsible for implementation and enforcement? How will the policy be communicated in plain English? Will there be an override process for the policy?

3. **Use a policy design process:** A reasonable policy should be designed to support contemporary learning so that innovative practices by individual teachers and school staff in general will not be curtailed. Design process engages stakeholders, responds to organizational goals, delineates guiding principles, maximizes opportunities, and guides implementation.

CORWIN
A SAGE Company

Helping educators make the greatest impact

CORWIN HAS ONE MISSION: to enhance education through intentional professional learning.

We build long-term relationships with our authors, educators, clients, and associations who partner with us to develop and continuously improve the best evidence-based practices that establish and support lifelong learning.

Solutions you want. Experts you trust.
Results you need.

Author Consulting

On-site professional learning with sustainable results! Let us help you design a professional learning plan to meet the unique needs of your school or district. www.corwin.com/pd

Institutes

Corwin Institutes provide collaborative learning experiences that equip your team with tools and action plans ready for immediate implementation. www.corwin.com/institutes

eCourses

Practical, flexible online professional learning designed to let you go at your own pace. www.corwin.com/ecourses

eLibraries

Your online professional resources library. Create a custom collection with more than 1200 eBooks and videos to choose from. www.corwin.com/elibraries

Read2Earn

Did you know you can earn graduate credit for reading this book? Find out how: www.corwin.com/read2earn

Contact an account manager at (800) 831-6640 or visit **www.corwin.com** for more information